THE BATTLE OF LAKE ERIE

In 1812 the United States declared war on Great Britain and sent three armies north to invade Canada. All three failed, and the one intended to capture the western part of what today is Ontario also lost Detroit to the British. Armed British ships on Lake Erie then were able to move troops and supplies easily along the American shore; and as a result the Americans could not recapture Detroit or again launch an attack on western Canada. President James Madison decided late in 1812 to build a United States naval squadron that would take control of Lake Erie; work on the ships began that winter. The following spring and summer the men of the squadron were assembled, organized, and trained. At the same time the British squadron was strengthened and made ready to fight. The two met on September 10, 1813, in the Battle of Lake Erie, a battle that decided the future of the section of the United States that lies between the Ohio River and the Great Lakes.

PRINCIPALS

OLIVER HAZARD PERRY (1785–1819), U.S. Navy officer who organized and commanded the American squadron on Lake Erie, a man with little battle experience but great drive.

ROBERT HERIOT BARCLAY (1784–1837), British commander on Lake Erie, an experienced naval officer and a veteran of the Battle of Trafalgar, where he had lost an arm.

DANIEL DOBBINS (1776–1856), merchant captain on the Great Lakes who helped to convince President Madison that the United States must build a squadron on Lake Erie. The President then gave him a warrant as a sailing master in the navy and put him in charge of building the ships.

JESSE D. ELLIOTT (1782–1845), U.S. Navy officer who had been in command on Lake Erie before Perry arrived there and who was second-in-command to Perry during the Battle of Lake Erie, even though he was slightly older than Perry.

WILLIAM HENRY HARRISON (1773–1841), American general who took command of the army in the western area after its first defeat. A former governor of Indiana Territory, he later became ninth President of the United States.

"*Perry Transfers to the Niagara,*" *from A History of Michigan in Paintings.*
(Courtesy, © *Michigan Bell Telephone Co.)*

A FOCUS BOOK

The Battle of Lake Erie, September, 1813

The Naval Battle That Decided a Northern U.S. Boundary

by James P. Barry

Illustrated with contemporary prints

FRANKLIN WATTS, INC.

575 Lexington Avenue   New York, N.Y. 10022

The authors and publishers of the Focus Books wish to acknowledge the helpful editorial suggestions of Professor Richard B. Morris.

Contents

THE BATTLE OF LAKE ERIE

A painting of Oliver Hazard Perry by J. W. Jarvis in the U.S. Naval Academy Museum. (U.S. Navy)

September 10, 1813

Early in the morning of September 10, 1813, the nine-ship American squadron lay at Put-in-Bay on Lake Erie. A light breeze rippled the water. At five o'clock a lookout at the masthead of the flagship *Lawrence* sighted the sails of the approaching British fleet, borne along by the morning wind from the southwest. Lieutenant Dulaney Forrest went below to rouse the American commander, Master Commandant Oliver Hazard Perry — by courtesy title, commodore. (In the navy, now as then, an officer who commands a ship is called captain, even though he actually holds a lower rank, and an officer who commands a squadron is called commodore. These are known as courtesy titles.)

Perry, who was sick and feverish, dressed, putting on the blue jacket of an ordinary seaman so that he would not attract the eye and aim of some sniper in one of the enemy fighting tops. The twenty-eight-year-old Perry, a brisk, determined young man with a tendency to plumpness, went on deck and gave orders for his squadron to get under way. At first the British commander, Robert Heriot Barclay, had that most important advantage in the days of sail — the weather gauge; that is, his vessels were upwind from Perry's and thus were far more maneuverable. Hence Barclay could take the initiative. Perry had to wait for him, but he impatiently put out small boats in an attempt to tow the American vessels into action. At 10:00 A.M. the wind shifted to the southeast. Now it was Perry who had the weather gauge. He moved out to battle.

Perry's famous blue flag now reposes in Memorial Hall at the U.S. Naval Academy, Annapolis, Maryland. (U.S. Navy)

As soon as Perry could identify the individual British vessels, he formed his line so that each of his ships would be opposite her assigned enemy. He then had the crew of the *Lawrence* assembled on the quarterdeck and ordered the battle flag run up. This was a large blue flag he had had made; on it were sewn crude letters reading "Don't give up the ship," the dying words of Perry's friend Captain John Lawrence, for whom the flagship was named. As the flag was hoisted the men gave

[4]

three cheers, which were repeated along the whole line. Then Perry ordered a double issue of grog and briefly went below to see that documents and letters were wrapped in a weighted package that could easily be dropped overboard if capture became imminent. This he turned over to the surgeon, Dr. Usher Parsons, whose station was belowdecks in the cockpit (the ship's hospital). On his return to deck, Perry had the drums and fifes call all hands to their battle stations.

So began a battle involving no more than a thousand men commanded by two relatively junior officers. A little over a month later in the Battle of Leipzig, 500,000 men were involved and the commanders were exalted personages. Yet the two battles were almost equally decisive.

The War of 1812

Ever since the American Revolution, feelings had been strained between Great Britain and the new United States. In 1803, Britain had declared war on Napoleon, and the British Royal Navy had blockaded the ports in Europe that were controlled by France. This blockade kept neutral ships from taking cargoes into French ports, and among the neutral ships were those from the United States. American shipowners and merchants were annoyed when their ships and cargoes were turned back, and angered when they sometimes were taken into British ports, where they might be sold.

The Royal Navy also insisted on searching U.S. merchant vessels on the high seas and impressing U.S. sailors (forcing them to join the British service) on the claim that they were deserters from the Royal Navy. In 1807 a British warship attacked a smaller American warship, the U.S.S. *Chesapeake*, and after killing three men and wounding eighteen, took off by force four U.S. Navy seamen who actually had deserted from the Royal Navy and enlisted in the U.S. Navy. Because of this incident war almost flared between the two countries, but responsible men on both sides managed to prevent it. In 1811 an American warship attacked a smaller British warship, mistakenly thought to have impressed a U.S. sailor, and battered her into submission, killing nine men and wounding twenty-three. The situation between the two countries on the high seas now became explosive.

During these same years, there were many people in what were then the western parts of the United States (Michigan, Indiana, Ohio, and Kentucky) who felt that the United States should seize Canadian territory. Americans had been pushing westward, fighting the Indians for their lands; to these people, it seemed equally reasonable to push north and take Canada away from the British. The troubles with the British at sea made such demands seem even more reasonable. The United States, despite the fact that its army was small and badly trained, began to make plans for invading its northern neighbor. On June 1, 1812, President James Madison sent Congress a message asking for war. Congress approved, and on June 19 the President signed a formal proclamation declaring war against Great Britain.

The United States planned to send out three armies, one to capture Montreal, one to capture Niagara, and one to capture what is today the western part of the Province of Ontario, opposite Detroit. None of these armies succeeded, but the one that was to seize western Ontario came to the most grief. The United States had no real force at Detroit and so Brigadier General William Hull was sent off to that frontier town with a regiment of U.S. regular soldiers and three regiments of militia, soldiers enlisted by the individual states for short periods. As it turned out, instead of capturing part of Canada, Hull lost Detroit.

On July 12, General Hull did cross the Detroit River and move into the little Canadian village of Sandwich without a fight. Hull was not a very adept general, however. He had had some experience fighting during the Revolutionary War, though not as a general, and he had had none since. He did not know what to do. He had some twelve hundred soldiers, most of whom were not well trained. The British at nearby Fort Malden had fewer but better soldiers, and the fort itself was a strong one.

General Hull dithered: Should he attack Fort Malden or should he not? He made some preparations to attack, but took no firm action. Then he learned that the British had captured the small American fort at Mackinac, farther to the west. (The U.S. commander at Mackinac never had been notified that there was a war.) At the same time the Wyandot Indians who lived near Detroit, and who had been friendly to the Americans, moved across the river and camped at Amherstburg, near Fort Malden. When he received a report that more British troops were coming to reinforce those at the fort, Hull led his men back again across the river.

The general wanted to pull back even farther, leaving Detroit entirely. The militia officers would not hear of this, however. The force stayed at Detroit, but about half of the best men were sent out to meet and guard a supply train that was coming north around the end of Lake Erie. At the same time, the British reinforcements arrived on the other side of the river. There were only 50 British regulars and 250 Canadian militia, but they were led by Major General Isaac Brock, a bold and experienced officer.

The day after he arrived, Brock sent a message to Hull demanding that he surrender. Using what today would be called psychological warfare, Brock wrote that once a battle started he could not be responsible for what was done by the Indians fighting with him. General Hull

[7]

The surrender of General William Hull in August, 1812. (Library of Congress)

sent back a refusal to surrender, but then he began to think of all the stories he had heard of Indian massacres and tortures. As darkness fell, he brought all of his men in to protect the town and fort at Detroit, leaving unguarded the narrowest place in the river, about three miles away.

That night about six hundred Indians did cross the river at that place, and at daybreak seven hundred British troops followed. General Brock had put as many old red coats on his militiamen as he could find, so that from a distance he seemed to have far more trained British regulars than was the fact. He also had his units advance in such a way that there was twice the usual space between them; as a result, his small force looked much larger than it really was. As this impressive-looking British force moved toward Detroit, and as the Indians appeared on the edges of the town, the British cannon across the river began to fire into the fort. General Hull soon ran up the white flag of surrender.

Mr. Madison's Decision

Instead of capturing the western part of Upper Canada, as Ontario then was called, the United States had lost the eastern part of Michigan. Now the British were able to use Detroit as a base from which to send out military forces to attack U.S. forts and supply depots. The British had three warships on Lake Erie, plus the U.S. brig *Adams* which they had captured at Detroit. The United States had no warships on the lake. As a result, the British could carry their troops to any place they wished along the American shore and no one could stop them. Even more important, they could bring supplies and weapons by water to Fort Malden and Detroit. In those days the roads in the west, both in

Canada and in the United States, were very bad, and the side that could move supplies by ship had a great advantage.

This British advantage, gained by controlling Lake Erie, seriously hindered Major General William Henry Harrison, who had taken over the American army in the West. Harrison, a former regular army officer who had become governor of the Indiana Territory, was one of

Map of Lake Erie and environs, showing battle areas.

the few soldiers in whom the people of the western area had confidence. They appointed him a major general in the Kentucky state militia so that he would have greater rank than the elderly Brigadier General James Winchester, a man similar to Hull, whom the federal government had placed in command. Without much trouble, Harrison persuaded Winchester to devote his time to recruiting; this left Harrison free to command the army in the field.

General Harrison carried out several small campaigns against the British and their Indian allies led by the chief Tecumseh. These all were in United States territory, however, not far from the western end of Lake Erie. Harrison's real purpose was to retake Detroit and then move on to another attack against western Canada. But the British advantage was so great that he was kept busy fighting the British on his own ground and could not move against Detroit. Finally Harrison wrote to the secretary of war, William Eustis, saying that the first step the United States must take was to seize control of Lake Erie.

In September of 1812, three men called upon President Madison in Washington. One of them was William Eustis. Another was Daniel Dobbins, a veteran captain of merchant ships on the Great Lakes. The third was Colonel Lewis Cass, one of the officers who had been with General Hull at Detroit, but who had been away meeting the supply train when Hull surrendered. These three men told the President that the United States must build a fleet on Lake Erie, so that they could take control of the lake. Dobbins recommended the town of Erie, Pennsylvania, as the best and safest place to build the ships.

After some discussion, President Madison decided that these men were right. A fleet must be built on the lake. He gave Daniel Dobbins a warrant as a sailing master in the navy and directed him to build four vessels at Erie.

[11]

Lieutenant Elliott, U.S.N.

The officer first placed in command on Lake Erie was Lieutenant Jesse D. Elliott. Elliott set up his headquarters at Black Rock, near Buffalo, at the Lake Erie end of the Niagara River. Meanwhile Daniel Dobbins had hired a number of ship carpenters on the Atlantic coast and had gone with them to Erie, Pennsylvania, where the Lake Erie ships were to be built. One of the first things he did after his arrival there was to write to Elliott, telling him his plans and asking if Elliott had any further instructions.

The reply probably made Dobbins swear. Elliott wrote, "It appears to me utterly impossible to build gunboats at Presq'isle." (Erie was called Presq'isle at that time.) Then the letter went on to say that, because of what he had heard "from persons who have long navigated the lake," he believed the only harbor on Lake Erie where naval vessels could be fitted out was the one where he was then located, at Black Rock. Dobbins, who had sailed on the Great Lakes for years and who knew them well, fired back a letter disagreeing strongly with what Elliott said. The lieutenant did not bring up the subject with Dobbins again.

In the harbor at Black Rock was a shipyard, and there, under Lieutenant Elliott's eye, ship's carpenters who had come from New York worked at converting four merchant vessels into fighting ships. Across the Niagara River was the British post of Fort Erie; cannon there were able to fire into the Black Rock shipyard, and as a result some of the carpenters quit and went home. But the work on the merchant vessels continued.

It was on October 2, 1812, that Jesse Elliott wrote his letter to Daniel Dobbins. The dashing Elliott had other things on his mind,

Daniel Dobbins. (Public Archives of Canada)

Old plan of the British post at Fort Erie on the Niagara River. Black Rock ship-yard was located just across the river.

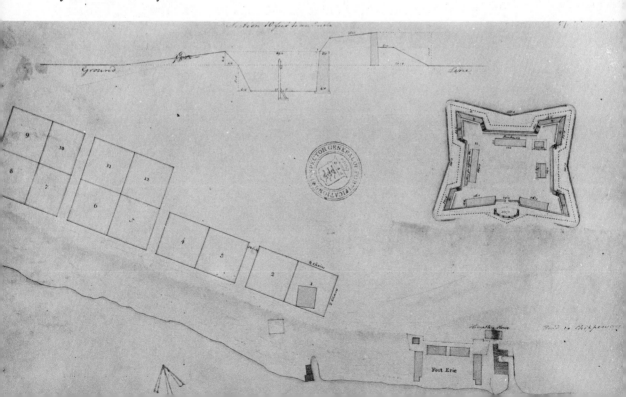

however. On the night of October 9 he led a few men in small boats across the Niagara River to Fort Erie. There, under cover of darkness, they boarded and captured two British vessels anchored under the guns of the fort; in trying to get one of them away, they ran her aground and had to burn her to prevent the British from recapturing her, but the other they towed back across the river with their rowboats to the U.S. side. She was the *Caledonia*. She joined the four U.S. vessels that were already in the Black Rock shipyard. Because of Lieutenant Elliott's courage during this raid, Congress awarded him a fine engraved sword. Elliott must have savored the feeling that he was now officially recognized as a hero.

Preparations for Battle

At Erie, Daniel Dobbins pushed ahead steadily. He built a shelter that his men could work under in bad weather. He also built a blacksmith shop, even though the iron he needed came slowly from Pittsburgh and he had to send to the Pennsylvania settlement of Meadville — some fifty miles south through the forests — to get steel for axes and other tools. But he was able to find many kinds of good shipbuilding timber near Erie. He hired local men to cut down trees and to haul logs out of the forests, using oxen or horses. The logs were then laboriously sawed by hand into planks, or were shaped by hand to make the larger wooden parts of the vessels.

Trees were paid for at the rate of one dollar each. (In those days a dollar was considered the day's wage for a skilled laborer.) After the axmen had gone through a woodlot, another man would follow later and count the number of trees cut. One receipt, issued the following

[14]

June to a widow named Lowrey, reads, "Gune the 25, 1813 trees cut on the widdo Lowreys plantation for ship timber twenty five counted by me Hugh McElroy."

By the middle of December, Dobbins had two 50-foot ships partly finished. During January, 1813, a number of his workmen became sick and one of them died. It is not known exactly what the disease was; Dobbins wrote simply that his men had "the sickness." Some men deserted him during the cold weather. But through the winter other shipwrights came in from the Atlantic coast, and finally, in early March, Noah Brown arrived. Brown had had much experience in his own shipyard in New York and he became superintendent of construction at Erie. After that, the actual building of ships went on more quickly, and Dobbins, who now could trust Brown to do that part of the job, was able to spend more of his time trying to get the supplies that were needed.

The business of bringing in supplies was the biggest problem of all. These ships were being built in the wilderness, far from the cities of the eastern states. Roads were bad even between such places as New York and Philadelphia. West of the big cities, however, they became even worse; so, whenever it was possible, heavy loads were moved by water. Some of the cannon that were to arm the Lake Erie ships came from New York, up the Hudson and Mohawk rivers, along Lake Ontario, over the road that ran along the Niagara River between Lakes Ontario and Erie, and in this way reached the U.S. naval yard at Black Rock. There Daniel Dobbins had to take over and move the guns on to Erie. During the winter months, teams of oxen and horses (whichever he could hire from the local settlers) pulled wagons and sleds to Erie. Often they came over the ice of frozen Lake Erie, loaded with big guns, anchors, and other supplies.

[15]

Early in the spring, Dobbins made one of his trips from Buffalo to Erie in an old open boat, carrying two heavy cannon and some other supplies. The boat had four oars and one sail. He could see British ships cruising on Lake Erie, so he followed the American shoreline as closely as he could. During the night a storm came up and he and his crew had a hard time keeping the boat from blowing ashore. The storm tossed her around considerably and did some minor damage, but after it had passed they discovered a much greater danger. The heavy weight of the guns, combined with the rolling of the boat, had opened her seams. She was leaking heavily and threatened to split open completely. Dobbins took a coil of rope, tied it fast at the bow, and wrapped it around and around the boat, heaving each turn of it as taut as possible. This kept her from coming apart. As daylight came they found themselves about ten miles from Erie — and they saw two British ships upwind. But the wind now was fair for them and they scooted on into the harbor at Erie without further trouble.

Guns also were hauled from as far away as Washington, D.C., over the mountains to Pittsburgh, and from there were taken north to Erie. That spring, as the winter thawed and the rivers filled with flood-water, crude keelboats could work their way north from Pittsburgh to within twenty miles of Erie. Such boats carried cannon and also many things that were made in Pittsburgh itself, such as rope for rigging, anchors, and cannonballs. Then Dobbins' wagons hauled these supplies overland to Erie.

By spring, six vessels were taking shape there. Four of them were relatively small, averaging perhaps 50 feet in length. Two of them were much bigger, between 100 and 110 feet in length. Because of the constant problems in getting enough iron from Pittsburgh, the vessels were fastened together in many places with wooden pins called treenails (and pronounced by shipbuilders as "trunnels"). And of course the

[16]

vessels were all made from green wood, cut directly from the forests. Normally, the best wood for shipbuilding was seasoned, that is, permitted to dry out for a number of months, before it was used. Ships made of green wood did not last as long as those made from seasoned wood. But as Noah Brown told his men, speaking about these vessels, "They will only be wanted for one battle; if we win, that is all that is wanted of them; if the enemy are victorious, the work is good enough to be captured."

Meanwhile, on the British side, in the naval yard at Malden, shipwrights were also at work. They had two main tasks. The first was to repair the British ships on Lake Erie and equip them for battle. Previously, these vessels had had no strong opponents on the lake and had been able to control it for the British. But they were old, not in the best repair, and not equipped with all of the cannon they would need in a major battle. The shipwrights at Malden had to make them ready for a real fight. The second job for these men was to build a new vessel, a full-rigged ship named the *Detroit*, which would be the flagship for the British squadron on Lake Erie.

The supplies needed to build and equip these British ships had to come over an even longer and much more difficult route than those for the American vessels. Cannon, anchors, rope, and cannonballs were brought by ship from England to Montreal; for none of these things was made in Canada. From Montreal they had to be pulled up the rapids of the St. Lawrence River in small boats. After that they were carried the length of Lake Ontario to Toronto (which then was called York). From there they were taken on, partly by land and partly by water, to Malden, across the river from Detroit.

An even worse complication from the British point of view was that the Americans had captured York and occupied it for a short time during April of 1813, and while they were there had carried off or

A view of Lake Erie at Amherstburg, near Malden, in 1813. (Public Archives of Canada)

destroyed many of the supplies that were on their way to Malden to outfit the British vessels on Lake Erie. The American raiders carried off twenty cannon and a great deal of ammunition. During the attack on York, a large supply of ropes, canvas, and other stores were burned. As a result, the British shipwrights at Malden never did get many of the supplies that they needed.

Master Commandant Perry, U.S.N.

At Newport, Rhode Island, there was stationed an energetic U.S. naval officer named Oliver Hazard Perry. His rank was that of master commandant, equal to the rank of commander in the U.S. Navy today.

He had heard about the preparations on Lake Erie, far away from Newport in the interior, and in September of 1812 he had written a letter to the secretary of the navy asking for service on the Great Lakes.

Perry came from a seafaring family. During the Revolutionary War his father, Christophers Raymond Perry, had sailed both on privateers and on a warship, and had twice been captured by the British and had twice escaped. The first escape was from a prison ship in New York Harbor; the second one, after eighteen months of confinement, was from a prison in Ireland. After the war, Christophers Perry became a merchant marine officer and then a merchant captain, sailing to Europe, South America, and the East Indies. This was a day when a single successful voyage could make a man's fortune; and Captain Perry had had a number of such voyages. But he remained interested in the navy and during the undeclared war between the United States and France in 1798, when the United States built several new warships, he accepted a commission as a navy captain and commanded a new frigate.

On one of his first merchant voyages after the Revolutionary War, Christophers Perry met a young passenger of Scottish background, Sarah Wallace Alexander. The following year they were married in Philadelphia. Oliver Hazard Perry was their first child. Altogether they had five boys and three girls; all of the boys became naval officers and two of the girls married naval officers. (One brother, Matthew C. Perry, was to become famous as the commanding officer of the naval expedition that first opened Japan to western trade.) Oliver Hazard was commissioned a lieutenant in the navy when he was seventeen years old. He served in the Mediterranean during the war with Tripoli, but he saw little fighting; part of the time he commanded a small schooner and part of the time he served in the U.S.S. *Constitution.*

Perry was eager to see action in this war, but at first there was no answer to his letter. Then in February of 1813 he received his orders;

A romanticized portrait of Oliver Hazard Perry. Perry, seated upon a sail and decked out in full uniform, seems unaware of the huge "Don't Give Up the Ship" flag flapping behind him. (Library of Congress)

he was to take about 150 of the best men of his command at Newport and proceed to the Great Lakes. Perry hurried on ahead of his men to Erie, where Daniel Dobbins was building the ships, and arrived there during the middle of March. With him he brought his thirteen-year-old brother, James Alexander, a midshipman. At that time there was no naval academy for young men to attend while they were training to become naval officers. Instead, they were appointed midshipmen and then served on active duty in the navy until they had learned their profession well enough to be commissioned. At Erie, James Alexander helped his older brother by doing many kinds of errands for him, at the same time learning at firsthand the problems of building and equipping ships.

Some one thousand untrained but eager militia drawn from the wilderness settlements nearby arrived at Erie late in March. In early April, Perry helped them to build two gun emplacements overlooking the harbor, and to mount three cannon in one of them and four in the other. They also built a few other small defenses that would help if the British attacked Erie.

Oliver Perry threw his energies into the job of outfitting the new ships, traveling to Pittsburgh to arrange for supplies that ranged from cables to cooking equipment. As his men arrived, he put them to work finishing construction and getting the ships fitted out for combat. On the fifteenth of April the first two gunboats, the *Tigress* and *Porcupine*, were launched at Erie, and on the first of May a third one, the *Scorpion*, slid into the water. The American squadron was beginning to take shape.

Lieutenant Barclay, R.N.

Lieutenant Robert H. Barclay, Royal Navy, arrived on the British side of Lake Erie on June 1, 1813, to take command of the squadron there. He had accepted this job after another officer had refused it because of the poor quality of the ships and the lack of sailors to man them. Barclay found a general lack of supplies of every kind, and there was little chance that any more supplies would reach Amherstburg. He had to organize his squadron as best he could, moving sails and equipment from one ship to another so that each of them would have a reasonable share.

Barclay was an experienced officer who had lost an arm at the Battle of Trafalgar between the British and French navies in October of 1805. He had been a lieutenant for some years and was nearing the time for his promotion to the rank of commander; he was in fact promoted several months after the battle. In many ways he had more experience than Perry, his opponent, but perhaps because his supply problems were so great, he did not always act with the energy and drive that Perry showed in everything he did.

Perry Consolidates His Squadron

Toward the end of May, Perry and Dobbins made a fast trip to Lake Ontario, traveling by boat, on foot, and on horseback. There they took part in the attack by American forces against the British Fort George, which stood on the Canadian side of the Niagara River where it entered Lake Ontario. On May 27 the British withdrew from the fort, leaving it to the Americans. The British forces along the entire

A portrait of Lieutenant Robert Barclay, Royal Navy, British commander at the Battle of Lake Erie. (Public Archives of Canada)

Niagara River were all pulled back at the same time. This move included the troops that garrisoned Fort Erie, opposite the Black Rock shipyard.

As a result, the guns of Fort Erie no longer prevented the American ships at Black Rock from moving out into Lake Erie. Perry immediately decided to transfer these vessels. As long as part of them were at one place and part at another, there was always the chance that the British, with a smaller force, could destroy each part separately. Once Perry could bring the two halves of his command together, his ships could only be destroyed in a major battle. After the capture of Fort George, he returned quickly to Black Rock. There he gave orders to take the guns from the defenses of the navy yard and mount them on the vessels. He rushed the men to carry supplies aboard. By June 6 the ships were ready.

Black Rock was on the upper part of the Niagara River, near the place where Lake Erie enters it. A swift current runs in the river there and sailing vessels could not move against it. Perry needed a week to haul the vessels up to Buffalo, on Lake Erie, with oxteams, sailors, and two hundred soldiers struggling along the riverbank, heaving on the towropes. It was not until June 13 that the last vessel was pulled clear of the rapids, and the squadron was ready to put out into Lake Erie.

Barclay had considered blockading Black Rock and Buffalo, stationing ships off the entrance to the river to prevent the American vessels from leaving. He decided that he did not have enough ships to do this, however. Instead, British vessels patrolled Lake Erie constantly. Several of them were large and heavily armed; those from Black Rock were small and had few guns. If they met, the British would almost certainly destroy the American ships.

Perry had to get the American ships to his base at Erie, and if possible he had to avoid meeting the superior British force while he made the move. On the evening of the thirteenth he sailed; he would make as much of the passage as he could by dark. But a strong wind made him return to Buffalo.

On the evening of the fourteenth he sailed again. The winds were still difficult, and he knew that the British ships were on the lake. He had to move slowly and the voyage took several days. Off Dunkirk, New York, the wind was light against him. A fog came down, so he anchored close to shore, using the fog as a curtain to hide him from his enemies. While he was anchored there a local man came aboard and said that he had been able to see both squadrons simultaneously from an intermediate point; he then told Perry which way the British had gone. With this information, Perry continued the game, and finally, on the morning of June 19, he brought the five vessels safely into the harbor at Erie. Thus Barclay had missed his first real opportunity to damage Perry's force.

Perry's Squadron Crosses the Sandbar

The two largest ships of Perry's squadron — both between 100 and 110 feet long — were the *Lawrence* and the *Niagara*. Noah Brown launched the first of these toward the end of June and the second early in July. While work on the ships was going forward very well, Perry now found he did not have enough men to crew them. He still had a total of only about 150 seamen. The 200 soldiers who had helped bring the Black Rock ships to Erie had returned to their military station near Buffalo and so he had no more use of them. As naval districts were then structured, Perry came under the commander on Lake Ontario, Commodore Isaac Chauncey, who felt that his own area was the most important one and that he could spare few men for Lake Erie. Chauncey had

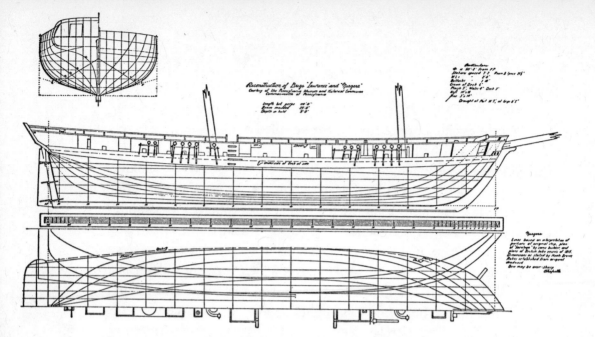

Reconstruction of lines of brigs Lawrence *and* Niagara. *(Reproduced from* History of the American Sailing Navy *by Howard I. Chapelle, courtesy of* W. W. Norton & Co.)

agreed earlier that Perry needed over 700 seamen, but when the time came he did not provide them.

Fortunately, soon after the middle of July, 75 seamen arrived at Erie. Toward the end of the month, 60 additional came in. Meanwhile, Lieutenant John Brooks of the Marine Corps (son of the governor of Massachusetts) arrived, and he managed to recruit about 40 men at Erie and Pittsburgh. Perry himself set up a recruiting station and enlisted in the navy about 100 men from the nearby frontier settlements.

In July, plentiful supplies of iron finally arrived at Erie. By then, however, it was too late to make nails or other ship fastenings out of the iron; but the blacksmiths set to work fastening such important items as boarding pikes — sharp tools on long handles which served both as weapons and as boathooks when vessels were engaged in close combat.

The iron scraps that were left over by the blacksmiths were carefully thrown into a pile. Later, such scraps were sewn into cloth bags to be fired from the cannon, in this way serving to cut the rigging and sails of the enemy ships and to wound their crews.

After they were launched, the vessels were rigged as they stood in the harbor; but their sails had to be made indoors. Normally this was done in a sail loft, a building where large pieces of canvas could be spread out on the floor and then cut and sewn. However, there was nothing of this kind in the little village of Erie, and so the local courthouse was turned into a sail loft. There the sails of Perry's squadron were completed at about the same time as the ships were launched.

As naval construction went forward at Erie, a number of men from Buffalo and Erie who owned small sailing vessels, some of them mere open boats, began to bring in supplies unofficially. They were encouraged by the high prices they could get from Perry's men and from the militiamen for goods that were not regularly available at Erie. In order to avoid the British ships that patrolled Lake Erie they traveled as much as they could by night. Their craft were so small that when the enemy did appear, the craft could easily dodge into the little coves and river mouths along the shore, and in this way escape.

British vessels often sailed outside Erie Harbor and were able to look in at what Perry was doing there. Sometimes only one of them would appear, sometimes Barclay's whole squadron. On July 21 the entire British squadron approached the harbor quite closely. Several of Perry's small gunboats, which were armed with one or two large cannon, fired from the harbor at the British vessels and the British returned a few shots, but no damage was done on either side. After a while Barclay's vessels sailed away.

Even though he was short of men, Perry drove ahead, getting his ships ready. His next big task was to move the ships built at Erie out across the sandbar that divided the outer harbor from the inner one. This was a particularly hard thing to do with the two largest vessels, the *Lawrence* and *Niagara*. First the *Lawrence* was to go across. Daniel Dobbins carefully checked the depth of water. Then he took charge of the vessel and moved her carefully to a position just inside the sandbar, anchoring her there.

This was a dangerous time, for the Americans could not defend themselves easily if they were attacked while crossing the bar. A British strike at this point could easily destroy the whole U.S. naval force on Lake Erie. In order to make some defense in case of such an attack, Perry had the *Niagara* anchored a little distance away inside the bar with her port (left) side toward the open lake, so that her guns on that side would help to protect the *Lawrence* while she was helpless. The smaller vessels were arranged in a similar manner so that they could help in the defense if necessary.

Then men swarmed over the *Lawrence*, taking off her guns and lowering them into small boats to be carried ashore, and removing all her equipment so that she rode as high out of the water as possible. In three hours they had stripped her of everything that could be removed. Then two large scows were brought out and one was placed on either side of her. These were inventions of the master builder Noah Brown, who referred to them as "camels." Each was about 90 feet long and 40 feet wide. They were built with holes in their bottoms that were fitted with plugs which could easily be removed or replaced. First the plugs were taken out and the camels were allowed to sink. Then seamen and shipwrights fastened them tightly to the vessel with ropes, wedges, and timbers. The plugs were then put back in their holes and men set to work laboriously pumping out the water by hand. As the camels slowly became lighter, they rose. As they rose in the water, they also buoyed up the ship that was lashed between them.

[28]

While all of this was going on, however, an easterly wind sprang up. It blew steadily. As a result, as though a tide had gone out, water over the sandbar became shallower. Dobbins had taken soundings the day before to measure the depth, and he had fastened the camels to the *Lawrence* in such a way that they would lift her easily over the bar with that depth of water. Now, however, the water level had dropped. The ship, even with the camels lifting her up, still lay too deep to be floated over the sandbar. The upshot was that they had to do the whole difficult job over again, sinking the camels lower than before, fastening them once more to the ship, and pumping them out. With the men working day and night, two days later the *Lawrence* finally moved slowly over the bar. And so far no British vessels had appeared.

Early in the morning the *Lawrence* was towed to the outer anchorage by rowboats. Under Perry's supervision, men immediately began to replace all of her guns and gear. By two o'clock in the afternoon everything was rerigged and her gun crews fired a triumphant salute. Then the *Niagara* moved up to the channel entrance and, as with her sister ship, men began to lighten her and to move the camels into place beside her. Meanwhile the wind shifted into the west and the water came back over the bar. The *Niagara* passed across it easily; by the next day she was floating outside, reequipped and ready for battle. No British vessels had yet appeared.

Finally the smaller vessels crossed the sandbar one by one. They were lightened, just as the big ones had been, by having their guns and equipment removed. But they did not need the camels; once they were free of all their heavy gear and arms they floated high enough in the water to float across. On August 4, Perry wrote to the secretary of the navy that his vessels were all outside the bar.

[29]

Problems on the British Side

The British had missed their best opportunity to destroy the American squadron. If they had attacked while Perry was crossing the bar, they would have had him at a great disadvantage. But they did not attack. Why? What had been happening on the British side?

Lieutenant Barclay was having even greater problems than Perry in assembling crews for his ships. During the month of July he had only 7 British seamen and 108 sailors of the Provincial Marine, the prewar British transport service on the Great Lakes, plus 160 soldiers on loan from the army. A few more soldiers and sailors were on their way to Fort Malden, but not many. Barclay was under the British commander on Lake Ontario, Commodore James Yeo, who, like Chauncey on the American side, felt that he needed most of his men in his own area.

British vessels had kept the harbor at Erie under observation while the American ships were building there. The British commander at Malden, General Henry Procter (who had replaced the vigorous General Brock, the man who had captured Detroit), made plans to attack Erie in a joint army and navy operation. But because Procter could not get enough troops from his superiors to satisfy him, he decided not to carry out his plan. Therefore it was left to Barclay and his undermanned ships to do something about Perry and his ships. Barclay had correctly decided that the best time to attack was when Perry was getting his vessels across the bar.

Barclay's ships first started patrolling off the harbor of Erie. But unaccountably, he and his squadron then went to Long Point, on the Canadian side directly across the lake from Erie, and remained there from July 29 to August 5. None of the official reports explains why.

During that time his vessels did not go near Erie. When he returned on the fifth, he saw that all of Perry's ships had crossed the bar. Perry's squadron was still in some disorder and was nearly as undermanned as Barclay's. Barclay did not, however, have his new flagship *Detroit*, which remained at Malden for lack of equipment and sailors. Barclay, who seems to have made the cautious decision, did not attack. Instead, he turned around and sailed back to Malden.

Perry Cruises the Lake

Commodore Perry, thinking that the British might be gathering at Long Point in order to launch an attack against Erie, decided to go there at once and see what they were doing. At 4:00 A.M. on August 6, he sailed away from Erie Harbor on his flagship, the *Lawrence*, taking with him all but three of his vessels. Two of the smaller ones he left behind — he had no crews for them — and a third, the *Amelia*, one of those refitted at Black Rock, had turned out to be too old and rotten for service and had been laid up.

When Perry arrived at Long Point he found nothing. The vessels swept along the coast for some distance, but there was no sign of British naval or military activity. They then headed back to Erie. Perry was satisfied now that there was no threat building up immediately across Lake Erie. His brief voyage had also tested the vessels and their equipment, and had enabled the crews to make necessary adjustments to ships and rigging. It also had given the crews some practice in working together.

During the next few days, the men loaded supplies and provisions aboard the ships. On the tenth there arrived from Lake Ontario ninety seamen, who were much better trained than the ones who had come earlier. Perry was happy to see them and their commander, Jesse Elliott, who had been on duty on Lake Ontario since Perry's arrival at Erie. The new men were distributed among the ships, including the two small ones that previously had no crews, and Elliott was given command of the *Niagara*. At about the same time, Perry received word that a number of his officers had been promoted and that Elliott too was now a master commandant. Thus Elliott was junior only to Perry and was the officer second in command of the U.S. squadron.

Several days later the entire squadron moved out of Erie and headed west. On the sixteenth they arrived at Sandusky Bay. As they approached it, a small, fast British schooner that had been scouting there went speeding off to Malden with word that the Americans had come. Next day General Harrison, U.S. Army commander in the West, with his staff and with some twenty Indian chiefs, came aboard. The cannon of the squadron fired a salute for Harrison, astonishing the Indians with the noise and smoke; after that they were shown the big ships and their big guns. While the chiefs were being taken over the vessels, Harrison and Perry conferred on future plans and decided that Put-in-Bay in the Bass Islands, a little distance offshore, was the best place for Perry's squadron to anchor.

After establishing himself at Put-in-Bay, Perry took his ships across the head of Lake Erie to Malden. There he cruised offshore, out of range of the artillery batteries of the fort, and studied the British vessels. He saw that the new *Detroit* had been rigged but had not yet joined the other five British vessels at anchor in the harbor. While Perry was making these observations, Barclay went to the highest house in Malden and from there studied the U.S. vessels through glasses. He noted that some of them maneuvered clumsily, and concluded that the men handling them were not yet adequately trained. In his mind he

[32]

began to form his plans for meeting the Americans in combat.

Perry brought his ships back to Put-in-Bay and had his men begin final preparations for battle. When they were working on the vessels he had them practice gunnery. But at this time many of the men were stricken with what was described as "bilious fever and dysentery." Today it might be called influenza or a virus infection. Apparently the new men brought it with them and it soon ran through the squadron. Many of the officers, including two of the surgeons, were sick with it. Perry himself contracted it and was seriously ill for a week.

Daniel Dobbins, meanwhile, was placed in command of the schooner *Ohio* and given the job of carrying supplies and messages from Erie to Put-in-Bay. It was not a dramatic assignment but it was an important one, and Dobbins' knowledge of Lake Erie made him the best man for it. He sailed back and forth, providing an essential link with the base at Erie.

On the last day of August, fifty volunteers from General Harrison's army came to the squadron. Many of them were boatmen from the western rivers, who thus had had some experience on the water. They were distributed among the vessels. On September 1, Perry felt well enough to take the deck and get the squadron under way for another visit to Malden. He sailed back and forth all day, noting that the *Detroit* was now at anchor with the rest of the British ships and apparently ready for battle. Barclay did not bring his ships out to meet Perry's, however; he had been promised more men from Lake Ontario and he wanted them on board before he went into a fight. Toward the end of the day Perry went home.

Now that the U.S. squadron was cruising Lake Erie, the British forces at Malden were in a bad situation. No supplies could move up Lake Erie to them. Not only were there British soldiers, sailors, and civilians at Malden to be fed, but General Procter had called upon

Tecumseh, the powerful Indian chief who had allied his people with the British, to provide warriors. They were to replace the soldiers Procter could not get from the British forces along Lake Ontario. The warriors came in to Malden, but they brought with them their wives and children, all of whom looked to Procter to feed them. The commissary general, the officer in charge of food supply, reported to General Procter on September 5 that he had on hand only two or three days' rations to feed more than 14,000 troops and Indians.

On September 6, Lieutenant Barclay's promised reinforcements arrived. He must have been sorely disappointed to find that there were only forty of them. He and Procter had constantly been discussing the urgent problem of supplies. Now Barclay decided that he had to go out with the men he had and fight the American squadron, hoping to defeat Perry and reopen the British supply line down Lake Erie. Procter agreed to give him some more soldiers to help man the ships.

At about this time, three men from Malden who favored the American cause made their way to the United States side and were quickly taken to Perry. From them he learned much about the British squadron, about its armaments, and about its officers. They told him also that Malden was running out of supplies and that Barclay soon could be expected to sail out in an attempt to clear the American squadron from Lake Erie.

The Two Squadrons

In the approaching battle there would be nine American vessels and six British. Those on the United States side ranged in size from the *Lawrence* and *Niagara*, each about 110 feet long, down to the little

50-footers built at Erie. The exact dimensions of each vessel are not known today, but there do exist records of their tonnages. A ton was considered to be 40 cubic feet of enclosed space. Tonnage was computed by formula, using measurements of the vessel. The two largest U.S. vessels measured 260 tons each; the *Caledonia*, next largest, 88 tons; the three smallest, 50 tons each.

The two large American vessels were brigs, two-masted square-riggers. The *Caledonia* was also a brig. With one exception the other American vessels were schooners, two-masted vessels with fore-and-aft sails; the exception was the *Trippe*, a sloop, having only one mast. Cannon at this time were rated by the weight of the solid shot that they fired; the *Lawrence* and *Niagara* each mounted two long 12-pound guns and eighteen of the short-range 32-pound carronades. The *Caledonia* had two long 24's and one 32 carronade. The smaller vessels had

Some gun types and carronades used in the American naval service from 1813 to 1815.

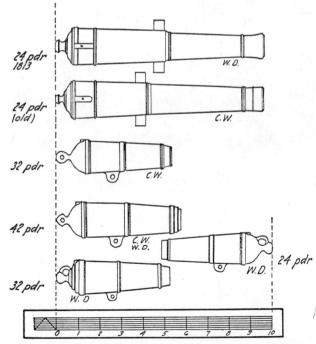

armament in proportion. Three of the little gunboats had single long 32's, the longest-range guns in the American squadron; two of them had no other weapons, but on the *Scorpion* there was also a 24-pound carronade. The *Trippe*, the most lightly armed of the American squadron, had only one long 24.

The British flagship, the *Detroit*, was about 125 feet long and she measured 300 tons. Next in size came the *Queen Charlotte*, of 200 tons, and then the *Lady Prevost*, of 96 tons. The smallest of the six British vessels, the *Chippewa*, measured only 35 tons. Thus the British squadron had both the largest and smallest vessels in the fight. The *Detroit* and *Queen Charlotte* were both ships, three-masted square-riggers. The *General Hunter* was a brig; the *Lady Prevost* has been called both brig and schooner; and the *Chippewa* was a schooner. The *Little Belt* was what the British called a cutter and the Americans a sloop — a single-masted vessel.

Barclay never did get his guns for the *Detroit*; she finally went into action with cannon taken from the walls of Fort Malden. The matches and ignition tubes available to him were so corroded and spoiled that the guns of his vessels had to be fired by the clumsy expedient of firing pistols into the vents. The *Detroit*, mounting borrowed armament, had a strange mixture of weapons: two long 24's; one long 18; six long 12's; eight long 9's; one 24-pound carronade; and one 18-pound carronade. At the time of the battle the *Queen Charlotte* mounted three long 12's and fourteen 24-pound carronades, and the *Lady Prevost* three long 9's and ten 12-pound carronades. The smaller British vessels had correspondingly lighter armament, the little *Chippewa* mounting only a single long 9-pounder. Although the six British vessels actually had more guns than the Americans — 63 as opposed to 54 — Perry's guns were considerably heavier. As a vessel normally presented only one side to an enemy at a time, her firepower was often

[36]

measured by the total number of guns that could be fired on one side at the same time; this was known as a broadside. The broadside firepower of the entire British squadron totaled about 460 pounds' weight of metal, that of the American squadron about 925.

All of these weapons were smoothbore muzzle-loaders. To load them it was necessary first to ram down the barrel a flannel bag holding gunpowder, then a wad, and then the cannonball or other projectile. Each item was thrust home solidly by several men using a long staff called a rammer. Then a priming rod was forced down into the vent on top of the breech in order to pierce the powder bag, and an ignition tube was inserted in the vent; this was a tube of tin filled with powder. The weapon then was pulled up into firing position using block and tackle so that its muzzle was sticking out the gunport in the side of the ship.

The cannon was fired by setting afire the powder in the ignition tube, using either a match — a sort of wick that burned with a steady glow — or a flintlock. The recoil from the firing carried the weapon backward into position for reloading. It then was swabbed out with a sponge on the end of a long staff similar to the rammer; this removed bits of burning powder or cloth and made it safe to ram in a new powder bag. A well-drilled gun crew could fire one shot a minute for short lengths of time.

Battle Is Joined

The night before the battle, Perry issued orders to his captains. The orders were written; in them he said that they were to keep their vessels within one-half cable length (about 300 feet) of each other during the battle. He told each of them which ship he was to oppose. His own *Lawrence* was to oppose the *Detroit*, Barclay's flagship; the *Niagara*, the *Queen Charlotte*; the *Caledonia*, the *Lady Prevost*. The smaller vessels were grouped. The *Scorpion* and *Ariel* were to meet the British *Chippewa*; the *Porcupine*, *Trippe*, *Somers*, and *Tigress* were to oppose the British *Hunter* and *Little Belt*. The British had superiority in long guns, the Americans in the shorter-range carronades. Therefore Perry directed his commanders to come in as close as possible to their opponents in order to get the full effect of their firepower. He quoted to them the words of Lord Nelson: "In case you lay your enemy close alongside, you cannot be out of your place."

As the two squadrons moved slowly toward each other that morning, Perry went about the deck of the *Lawrence*, once more inspecting each gun and giving each gun crew a word of encouragement or a joke. To some men who had served aboard the famous *Constitution* he spoke of their past exploits, and he called by their names the men of another crew, Rhode Islanders from his hometown of Newport. After his inspection, Perry waited, masking his impatience.

The commodore had with him on the quarterdeck his brother James Alexander and another young officer. It would be their duty in the thick of battle, when voice commands could not be heard for any distance, to run with messages to whatever part of the ship Perry needed to send an order. They too waited for the action to start.

The crews of Barclay's ships, because of the supply problems, were down to half rations on most kinds of foods and they did not have a single full day's supply of flour on board. Whiskey was a standard part of the ration in those days and it was usual for men to have a double issue of it before battle. The British supply was so low that the men had had to go without it for several days in order to have enough grog on hand for the day of the fight.

[38]

Old engraving shows Oliver Perry just before the Battle of Lake Erie, giving last-minute instructions to one of the Lawrence's gun crews. (Library of Congress)

Lake Erie was smooth and the breeze was light. For an hour and a half the squadrons maneuvered slowly toward each other. Decks were sprinkled and sanded so that blood would not make them slippery. No one spoke much; some of the men talked together quietly, telling each other what to do with their belongings if they were killed. As the two squadrons came nearer, most eyes were on the respective enemy. The British vessels kept close together, well under control. They had all been freshly painted, and their flags made bright spots of color in the sunshine. The larger American vessels were also grouped together, but some of the little gunboats were falling behind in the light and tricky wind; the *Trippe*, the last of the line, was almost two miles astern of the *Scorpion* and *Ariel*, which led the squadron.

As the two lines continued to approach each other, the command "Silence" was given on the *Lawrence*. Then there was no noise except when a command was given to trim sail and the bo's'n's pipe shrilled. All on board waited in suspense as the battle lines drew closer. The men could feel their hearts beating as they waited.

Map shows disposition of British and American squadrons at the beginning of the battle.

12 NOON

BRITISH

 CHIPPEWA DETROIT HUNTER CHARLOTTE PREVOST BELT

AMERICANS

 SCORPION ARIEL LAWRENCE CALEDONIA

 NIAGARA SOMERS PORCUPINE TIGRESS TRIPPE

A bugle sounded on board the British flagship *Detroit*; this was followed by cheers from all the crews of the vessels in the British line; then musicians played a few bars of "Rule Britannia." As the last note sounded, the *Detroit* fired one shot from a long 24-pounder, opening the battle. The distance between the two flagships still was a mile and a half, and the shot fell short. A few minutes later a long 24 fired again and this time the shot hit the *Lawrence*. At Perry's command, the U.S. gunboat *Scorpion* returned the fire with her long 32. Soon afterward Perry fired a broadside from the *Lawrence*, but the shots all fell short. Then he ceased firing and made all sail toward the enemy; he ordered word passed by speaking trumpet to the other U.S. vessels that they too were to close in.

The *Niagara* Lags Behind

While the long-range British guns chopped away at her, Perry's *Lawrence* moved steadily toward the *Detroit*. It took half an hour for her to close to the range of her shorter cannon. But Jesse D. Elliott's *Niagara* did not move in with the rest of the U.S. vessels. He shifted one of her bow guns over to the other side so that he could fire at the British with two long guns, but he stayed so far from his designated opponent, the *Queen Charlotte*, that she was unable to reach the *Niagara* with 24-pound carronades having a range of slightly over a thousand yards. Therefore, the *Charlotte* went ahead of the next ship in the British line and joined Barclay's *Detroit* in attacking the *Lawrence*.

The early exchanges caused damage on both sides. Two American vessels were in trouble; on the *Scorpion* one gun had burst, killing several of the crew, and then had fallen down a hatch, injuring some of

[41]

those below. On the *Ariel* a 12-pounder had burst. The British also had had a series of casualties. The captain of the *Queen Charlotte*, Robert Finnis, and his second-in-command were both killed early in the battle by American fire. A third officer was severely wounded. This left in command a Lieutenant Irvine of the old Provincial Marine, the prewar British transport service. He was brave, but he had had little training for battle.

Events on Perry's vessel were going grimly as the combined fire of the *Lawrence*'s adversaries began to knock her to pieces. David Bunnell, a seaman who had charge of one of the gun crews, suddenly was blinded and thought he had been hit; but then he realized that a man standing near him had been struck in the head by a cannonball and the man's brains had been plastered all over Bunnell's face. Then a British cannonball struck the muzzle of one of the guns near Bunnell, spraying little pieces of metal into the crew. Debris and wreckage were everywhere. The smoke from the cannon was so thick that all the men could do was fire straight ahead; they could see little, but the vessels were so close together that they could not miss.

About an hour and a half after the battle started, Barclay, the British commander, was wounded in the thigh. He was taken below, had his wound treated, and promptly returned to the deck. His flagship, the *Detroit*, showed the scars of American cannonballs but was still in much better condition than Perry's *Lawrence*.

On that vessel, Dr. Usher Parsons, belowdecks in the cockpit, was caring for the stream of wounded men who came below. The wounded complained to the doctor that the *Niagara* had not come up. "Why does she hang back so, out of the battle?"

Because of the *Lawrence*'s shallow draft, the cockpit was above the waterline and cannonballs crashed through the side of the vessel into it. Midshipman Lamb, who had come below with a fractured arm,

[42]

was struck by a cannonball and killed just as the surgeon finished splinting his arm. Charles Pohig, a Narragansett Indian who had enlisted with Perry and who was seriously injured, was also killed in the cockpit by a cannonball. The shots did less serious damage as well. One of them smashed into the closet where all of the chinaware had been stowed. The commodore's dog had hidden there from the battle; after the crash the dog set up an angry barking that lasted throughout the fight.

On deck, things were far worse. The Marine Corps lieutenant, John Brooks, as he stood talking to Perry, was suddenly knocked across the deck by a cannonball and mortally wounded. Blood, brains, hair, and bone fragments splattered the deck and the rigging. The *Lawrence*'s sails and rigging were afire. Her first lieutenant, John J. Yarnell, was wounded three times but always came back to the deck. Every officer aboard, except Perry and his brother, was either wounded or dead. And still Elliott's *Niagara* hung back. Men died asking the question, "Where's the *Niagara*?"

The Shattered *Lawrence*

Perry moved coolly through the chaos, directing his men and controlling their desperate efforts. He remained outwardly calm, no matter what he felt as he saw the enemy fire kill and maim the men he had trained. As the battle continued and men were needed desperately on deck, he brought up the surgeon's six assistants from the cockpit, one at a time. Then he asked if any of the wounded could pull a line, and two or three of them crawled feebly up from below to help. At 1:30 P.M., he called down the sailors and marines from the fighting tops to

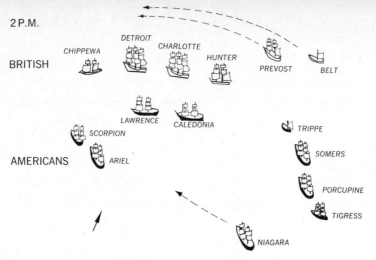

Map shows ship dispositions at approximately 2:00 P.M.

man the guns; the gun crews had been annihilated. By 2:30 not a gun on the *Lawrence* was in action.

The *Lawrence* was shattered. Her sails were so cut up by British shot that they could hold no wind. Twenty-two of her men were dead and sixty-one were wounded seriously. She could neither sail nor shoot. It seemed that the only thing left for Perry to do now was to strike his flag — the signal of surrender. Once that was done, according to the rules of warfare, he was technically a prisoner and could not leave his ship.

The *Lawrence* was out of action and obviously soon must strike her flag. At that point Elliott brought the *Niagara* up into close action.

Perry Changes Ships

Why had Elliott kept the *Niagara* out of action for so long? Why did he choose at this time to close with the enemy? Historians have argued the question ever since. Perhaps Elliott misunderstood his or-

[44]

ders; certainly he was no coward, though some on the *Lawrence* thought he was. Before Perry came to Lake Erie, Elliott had been in command there; he had led the daring raid on Fort Erie and he now wore the sword that Congress had given him to honor his courage then. Actually, he was more likely to be hungry for glory than scared of a fight. It is known, however, that his judgment was sometimes poor; after all, he had told Daniel Dobbins that ships could not be built at Erie.

It seems likely that Elliott *was* hungry for glory. But now he was second-in-command; if the battle was won as Perry had planned it, the chief honors would go to Perry no matter how bravely others fought. If Elliott let Perry's ship bear the brunt of the battle, however, until the commodore was killed or seriously wounded, or until he had to strike his flag and was out of the action, then Elliott could move in, assume command, and win the day.

No one knows exactly what Elliott thought; but as the *Lawrence* was about to strike her flag, Elliott moved the *Niagara* into battle. Perry saw her and immediately made a decision: He would move to the *Niagara*, take over command of her, and continue the fight. Quickly he ordered a small boat put over the side. It was manned by four oarsmen. He boarded it, and just before he pushed off, a soldier threw down to him his "Don't give up the ship" flag. The four oars bit into the water and the boat moved across the half mile that separated the two vessels, passing directly through enemy fire. Perry reached the *Niagara* unhurt; ten minutes later he saw the *Lawrence* strike her flag.

Perry was angry when he went aboard the *Niagara*. Elliott's greeting was the question, "How goes the day?" It was not soothing to the commodore and he replied curtly. Elliott quickly volunteered to go and bring up the lagging gunboats. Perry told him to do so. Elliott took Perry's boat and went off through the battle to fetch the smaller vessels.

[45]

Above, one of a number of fanciful pictures showing Perry transferring from the shattered Lawrence *to the* Niagara. *Sporting full uniform, Perry, clutching sword and battle flag, stands up in the boat as his younger brother presumably implores him to get down. Actually, there were only four oarsmen. Modern painting used as frontispiece of this book, showing Perry boarding the* Niagara, *comes closer to the truth. (Historical Society of Pennsylvania)*

"We Have Met the Enemy and They Are Ours"

Perry quickly looked about the *Niagara*. She was in good condition; little enemy fire had been able to reach her and most of her own supply of ammunition was unfired. Only one man aboard had been

[46]

killed and three wounded. Perry had his battle flag run up. Meanwhile the breeze was freshening and both squadrons moved ahead at increasing speed; as a result the *Lawrence* fell behind, drifting out of the battle. There was a momentary lull in the firing on both sides. The *Niagara* was now abreast of Barclay's *Detroit*. Behind the *Detroit* in the British line sailed the *Queen Charlotte*. The increasing breeze also helped the smaller U.S. gunboats to close the gap between themselves and the rest of the squadron. With Elliott commanding them, they moved into position and began to fire their heavy guns into the largest British ships.

Barclay saw what was happening on the American side and began to arrange a defense. But at this time he received his second wound of the battle. A shot struck the one-armed British commander in his good shoulder and totally disabled him. He was taken below for treatment.

At 2:45 P.M., Perry gave the signal for close action. Under all possible sail, with the wind still freshening, he bore down on the British

Old lithograph depicts Perry's victory on Lake Erie, after he had shifted his flag to the Niagara. Shattered Lawrence *is on the left. Plate represents position of the two fleets as the* Niagara *(center) is pushing through the enemy's line. (Library of Congress)*

line. The British vessels, seeing him come, tried hastily to maneuver out of the way. Instead, the *Queen Charlotte* fouled the *Detroit*, tangling with her rigging and fastening the two vessels together. The *Niagara* rushed toward them, passed within twenty-five yards of them, and fired her starboard broadside, raking the length of the two British ships. At the same time, she fired her port broadside into the *Lady Prevost* and *Chippewa*, raking both of those British vessels. She then luffed, spilling the wind from her sails, and remained in position to fire broadside after broadside into the two largest British ships. The smaller U.S. vessels also poured shot after shot into them from their heavy guns.

Damage to the *Charlotte* and *Detroit* was great. Their hulls were smashed and their sails and rigging hopelessly cut up. There were forty-two killed or wounded on the former and fifty on the latter. The American fire continued unrelentingly. Within fifteen minutes after the *Niagara* fired her first broadside, an officer appeared at the stern of the *Queen Charlotte*, waving a white flag fastened to a boarding pike.

Map shows positions of ships at about 2:50 P.M.

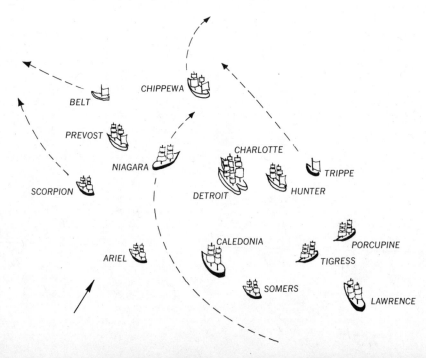

It was a signal of surrender, and the *Detroit* surrendered immediately afterward. Within moments all firing had ceased and all the British vessels had surrendered except two of the smallest, the *Little Belt* and the *Chippewa*; these tried to slip away but were intercepted by the *Scorpion* and the *Trippe* of the U.S. squadron. Sailing Master Champlin, who commanded the *Scorpion*, had fired both the first American shot and the final shot in the battle.

As the smoke drifted away from the scene, the two squadrons lay completely mixed together. Off to the eastward floated the disabled *Lawrence*. Near the battle area lay Western Sister Island. Perry took the time to write a brief message to General William Henry Harrison:

U.S. Brig *Niagara*, off Western Sister, head of Lake Erie, Sept 10, 1813, 4 P.M.
Dear General:
  We have met the enemy and they are ours. Two ships, two brigs, one schooner and one sloop.
Yours, with great respect and esteem,
O. H. Perry

He wrote a similar message to William Jones, secretary of the navy, and sent a boat to carry both messages ashore.

Around the entire lake, people had heard the fierce cannonading. Daniel Dobbins in the schooner *Ohio*, at anchor in the harbor at Erie, had heard it plainly. People along the Ohio shore heard it, and so had the British at Fort Malden and Detroit. But none of them knew yet who had won.

[49]

Another romanticized engraving of Perry at Lake Erie, presumably as British ships are surrendering. Men wave their hats in sign of victory as Perry himself aids a gun crew in sighting the weapon. Note rooster on gun carriage at right. (Library of Congress)

The Surrender

The Americans now took possession of the individual British ships. Crews from the U.S. vessels were put aboard each of the British ones. There they found tremendous damage, especially to the two largest ships. The commander and second-in-command of every British vessel had either been killed or wounded. The Americans had the task of guarding the prisoners and repairing the vessels of both squadrons sufficiently to get them back to harbor.

Once he saw these things begun, Perry returned at about four o'clock to his first flagship, the *Lawrence*. The deck was slippery with blood and brains, and twenty bodies were strewn among the wreckage. The groans of the wounded could be heard everywhere. As Perry came over the side, the few able men who remained approached him. For a long moment they faced each other silently, unable to speak. Several of the men shook his hand. Then he asked for his young brother James Alexander, who had remained on board.

No one had seen him. Had he been knocked overboard in the chaos of the battle? There was a general stir on the *Lawrence* as men went looking for him. They found him fast asleep in his berth, exhausted by the work and excitement of the day.

Perry then went to his quarters and changed from the seaman's jacket he had worn throughout the battle to his normal uniform. He went back to the deck. Soon the British officers, one from each vessel, came to surrender formally; Lieutenant O'Keefe, an army officer who had been on the *Detroit*, represented the wounded Barclay. They approached Perry, walking through the carnage, and extended the hilts of their swords toward him. Standing erect and speaking in a low tone, he refused to take the swords. He inquired for Barclay and the other

[51]

British wounded and said that he was sorry that he could offer them no medical help, for he had only one surgeon in the entire squadron who was well, and that one was overwhelmed with work. After the British officers left, Perry walked to the rail and for some time looked thoughtfully over the water.

General Harrison Crosses the Lake

The dead soldiers, sailors, and marines were lashed up in their hammocks, each with a roundshot at his feet, and committed to Lake Erie, while the chaplain, Thomas Breeze, read the burial service. At 9:00 A.M. on the morning of the eleventh, the combined squadrons stood into Put-in-Bay, where all vessels anchored. Repairs and cleaning-up continued throughout the day. Dr. Usher Parsons, the only doctor in the squadron who was not still terribly ill, had to care for the American wounded alone. He began his amputations on the *Lawrence* at daylight of the eleventh and finished them at 11:00 A.M. The less seriously wounded then kept him busy until midnight.

On the twelfth, Dr. Parsons moved on to the *Niagara*, where the wounded had lain until then without a surgeon's care. After giving them immediate attention, he had the most seriously injured moved to the *Lawrence*, where he could attend to them better. It speaks well for Dr. Parson's skill and care that of the ninety-six wounded Americans, only three died. The doctor modestly attributed the recovery of so many men to the fresh vegetables brought them by farmers along the Ohio shore, to fresh air, and to the happy mental state caused by victory.

Meanwhile, the officers of both squadrons were buried. At 10:00 A.M. the colors were run to half-mast, the bodies were lowered into boats, and the boats rowed slowly and solemnly to the shore while the ships fired minute guns. As they landed, a procession formed with the body of the youngest and least-ranking officer in the lead, alternating American and British, the body of Captain Finnis, commander of the British *Queen Charlotte*, coming last. The living British and American officers formed a column behind the bodies, alternating two British and two American, and slowly marched to funeral music played by the combined musicians of both squadrons. The bodies were lowered into the earth, the burial service was read, and a volley of musketry was fired over the graves.

The wounded of both squadrons were transferred to the *Lawrence*, where Dr. Parsons and the British surgeon, Dr. Kennedy, cared for them. Lieutenant Yarnell, the officer who had been wounded three times during the battle, was placed in command of her, and after repairs she sailed to Erie as a hospital ship. The wounded Barclay, commodore of the British squadron, was near death; Perry paroled him and arranged for him to be taken back as near as possible to the British forces on Lake Erie. Barclay survived and later was cleared of fault in his defeat by a court-martial in England.

The prisoners who were not seriously wounded were landed and were then marched to Chillicothe, then the capital of Ohio, by soldiers from General Harrison's army. Having taken care of the dead, the wounded, and the prisoners, Perry turned his energies to readying the vessels of both squadrons to carry Harrison's army across the lake for an invasion of Canada. The army was now camped at several places along the Ohio shore of Lake Erie, waiting for transport. Altogether Perry managed to prepare thirteen vessels of the combined squadrons, but even this number could move only a third of the army at one time. The troops were first carried by the vessels to Put-in-Bay. On September 20 they began to embark; by the twenty-fourth Harrison's entire force of 4,500 men were all safely landed there, except for a regiment of Kentucky cavalry — under Colonel Richard M. Johnson — that proceeded along the shore toward Detroit.

Additional boats were needed both to carry the troops in the final attack and to land them on the Canadian shore. The army had foreseen this need and during the previous winter and spring, while Dobbins and Perry were building ships at Erie, an army officer, Major Thomas S. Jessup, had supervised the building of large, open, flat-bottomed boats at Cleveland. By July 5 he had about seventy of them completed, ready for use by Harrison's force, and as soon as Perry's victory was complete they were brought to Put-in-Bay.

By the twenty-sixth, a second shuttle movement of the vessels had carried the army to Middle Sister Island, about twelve miles from the British Fort Malden. They were crowded together on this little island of only five or six acres. Meanwhile, Perry and Harrison sailed along the shore to the east of Malden in the U.S. schooner *Ariel* and chose a good landing place. On the twenty-seventh the whole force was crowded into the ships or into the boats that were towed by the ships; they sailed early in the morning with a fair wind and at 2:00 P.M. came to anchor a quarter mile off the designated landing beach. Perry assigned Jesse Elliott to control the landing; under Elliott's supervision a line of boats moved toward the shore, expecting to be met by fire from an enemy force hidden behind a small ridge a little distance away. In the bows of six of the boats were mounted cannon, loaded and ready to fire. It turned out that there was no enemy there, however, and the troops landed in good order without any opposition.

Scouts were sent out, local people were questioned, and it soon was evident that General Procter, the British commander, had pulled his army back from Fort Malden and was retreating inland. He had

[54]

General William H. Harrison, shown here at the Battle of Tippecanoe. (Library of Congress)

left only a rear guard to destroy the barracks, navy yard, and supplies. The squadron, towing the remaining boats, immediately got under way again, moved close to the fort, and landed the rest of the army without meeting any British defense.

The Battle of the Thames

Tecumseh and his Indian followers objected strongly to the retreat by Procter. There were not yet any Americans on Canadian soil when Procter began to withdraw; he had not yet been in any battle. The Indians could not see why he retreated and were astounded that he would not stand and fight. They felt that he was deserting them, and Tecumseh openly called him a coward. The chief did agree reluctantly, however, to go partway with the retreating British army, and a number of his best warriors went with him. The rest of the Indians scattered.

General Harrison assigned soldiers to garrison Detroit, Sandwich, and Fort Malden, to protect them if those scattered Indian allies of the British should return. This left him with slightly more than three thousand men with whom to pursue the retreating British force. By October 1, Colonel Johnson's regiment of mounted Kentuckians, who had crossed over near Detroit, also joined Harrison. The British meanwhile had retreated along the Detroit River and the shore of Lake St. Clair and had started up the river Thames, which empties into Lake St. Clair from the east, running parallel to the northern shore of Lake Erie. But the British rear guard failed to destroy the bridges behind them as they pulled back; and as a result the Americans reached the mouth of the Thames late on October 2.

While Harrison pursued the British army along the shore, Perry took his squadron by river and lake to the Thames's mouth. He was able to sail a little way up the river, but soon it became too shallow and narrow. Most of the navy people remained with their ships, but Perry, who had become good friends with Harrison, accompanied the troops throughout the action.

The retreating General Procter did not keep tight control of his forces. He had his family with him, and perhaps because of this he retreated faster than his army, on the pretext of looking for a good place to make a firm stand. The Americans followed quickly behind that army, however, and Procter at last was forced to choose a defensive position. It was not a particularly good one. He formed his troops hastily in two lines, between a large swamp on the right and the Thames River on the left. No earthworks were thrown up and no logs cut down for protection. Procter's Indian allies, under the chief Tecumseh, took position in the swamp.

General Harrison pressed on quickly. As his force approached the British defensive position, he held back his left flank from contact with the Indians in the swamp and ordered Johnson's Kentucky cavalry to charge in the center. The tired redcoats, unprotected by breastworks, got off only a scattered volley before the Kentuckians had galloped through both their lines. American infantry followed, surrounding small groups of the disorganized British. Meanwhile Colonel Johnson led his cavalrymen toward the Indians in the swamp. There they dismounted, moving in to fight the Indians on foot. After a hard fight in which Tecumseh was killed, the rest of the Indians fled.

The British lost some 630 killed or captured; 245 escaped and

[57]

Battle of the Thames, October, 1813. Action at center shows Colonel Johnson shooting Tecumseh who, having discharged his rifle, has just raised his tomahawk. On hill at upper left is General Harrison with Perry and General Cass, who acted as Harrison's aides during the battle. (Library of Congress)

made their way in time to the British forces on Lake Ontario. The Indians carried off all but 33 of their own dead. U.S. casualties were 7 dead and 22 wounded. It was a clear American triumph, one of the few American victories on land during the entire War of 1812.

The Results

Perry's victory was glorious news in the East. The President promoted him to captain in an order dated September 10, 1813. Congress awarded both Perry and Elliott gold medals, other officers of the fleet silver medals, midshipmen and sailing masters swords, and the sailors, marines, and soldiers of the fleet three months' pay. Congress also directed the President to buy the captured British vessels from their captors (who by custom now owned them) and for the purpose appropriated $225,000 in prize money to be distributed to those who took part in the battle, or to their heirs.

By his success, Perry destroyed British seapower west of Niagara. After Harrison's victory all of the western part of Upper Canada was in American hands. The British had lost the only good area from which they could move to seize Ohio and Michigan. Further, the retreat and final defeat of Procter and the death of Tecumseh greatly weakened the Indian ties with the British. The United States held Lake Erie and western Upper Canada for the rest of the war. British forces could reach Mackinac and the areas beyond via Georgian Bay or the Ottawa River, but they had lost their grip on the heart of the Northwest and the waterway that controlled it.

At the end of the war, the United States was not in a good bargaining position. The British had conquered Napoleon. They were able to send formations of experienced veterans to fight in Canada. British forces held Mackinac and Prairie du Chien. A British army had invaded and burned Washington. Thus the American representatives at the Treaty of Ghent had few trump cards. But the United States,

British and American diplomats signing the Treaty of Ghent, December, 1814. (Library of Congress)

thanks to Perry and Harrison, did hold most of Upper Canada west of Lake Ontario.

This strengthened the American negotiators enough so that they were able to stave off a British attempt to limit the sovereignty of the United States in Ohio and the area west of the Great Lakes. The British wanted to make those lands into an Indian country, where their savage allies could live and where U.S. pioneers would not be permitted to settle. In reply, the American representatives could point to an accomplished fact: the United States now held the western part of Upper Canada. It was hardly realistic to ask them to give up not only what they had won in battle but also territory that from the beginning they had considered their own. The British conceded the point. United States boundaries today along Lake Erie and to the westward are the result of Perry's brilliant victory.

A Selected Bibliography

Bunnel, David C. *Travels and Adventures*. Palmyra, N.Y.: J. H. Bortles, 1831.

Chapelle, Howard I. *History of the American Sailing Navy*. New York: W. W. Norton & Co., Inc., 1949.

——. *History of American Sailing Ships*. New York: W. W. Norton & Co., Inc., 1935.

Dobbins, Captain W. W. *History of the Battle of Lake Erie*. Erie, Pa.: Ashby Printing Company, 1913.

Dodge, Robert J. "The Struggle for Control of Lake Erie." *Northwest Ohio Quarterly*, XXXVI, 1964.

Dutton, Charles J. *Oliver Hazard Perry*. New York: Longmans, Green and Co., 1935.

Gooding, S. James. *An Introduction to British Artillery in North America*. Ottawa, Canada: Museum Restoration Service, 1965.

Hitsman, J. Mackay. *The Incredible War of 1812*. Toronto, Canada: University of Toronto Press, 1965.

Horsman, Reginald. *The War of 1812*. New York: Alfred A. Knopf, 1969.

Mahan, Captain A. T. *Sea Power in Its Relations to the War of 1812*, II. Boston: Little, Brown, and Company, 1905.

Mahon, John K. "British Command Decisions in the Northern Campaigns of the War of 1812." *Canadian Historical Review*, XLVI, 1965.

Manucy, Albert. *Artillery Through the Ages*. Washington, D.C.: U.S. Government Printing Office, 1949.

Parsons, Usher. *Battle of Lake Erie*. Providence: Benjamin T. Albro, 1853.

Paullin, Charles Oscar, Editor. *The Battle of Lake Erie*. Cleveland: The Rowfant Club, 1918.

Severance, Frank H., Editor. "The Dobbins Papers," *Publications of the Buffalo Historical Society*, VIII, 1905.

Stacey, C. P. "Another Look at the Battle of Lake Erie," *Canadian Historical Review*, XXXIX, 1958.

Index

ABOUT THE AUTHOR

James P. Barry graduated in 1940 from Ohio State University, with a B.A. in English (cum laude, with distinction, Phi Beta Kappa), and that same year entered the Army as a lieutenant of artillery. He served in the European theater of operations during World War II, then remained in the Army for over twenty-five years, finally leaving it as a colonel. During that time he served in many places, including a tour in the Pentagon as senior editor for the Director of Army Intelligence.

He has written a number of articles on military and historical subjects as well as a book of regional history, *Georgian Bay, the Sixth Great Lake* (Clarke, Irwin & Co., Ltd., Toronto). He also has written a general history of the Great Lakes region that is scheduled for fall, 1970, publication. He is married to a high school librarian and is an administrator at Capital University, in Columbus, Ohio.

11/16
3
6/07

11/27/23
4
7/12/19